Needlework Patterns
in the
Era of Jane Austen

Ackermann's Repository

OF

ARTS, LITERATURE, COMMERCE,

Manufactures, Fashions, and Politics

1809 - 1820

Designed and Edited by

Jody Gayle

📖 *Publications of the Past*

Publications of the Past, Inc.
PO Box 233
Columbia, MO 65205

For further information email
jody@jodygayle.com
or visit
www.JodyGayle.com

ISBN-13: 978-09884001-9-1

Acknowledgements

My sincerest gratitude to the Philadelphia Museum of Art Library for permission to reintroduce the two-hundred-year-old *Ackermann's Repository of Arts* to a whole new group of readers.

A special thank you to the authors of Regency era fiction, who have continued to make the society, customs and fashions of early nineteenth century England vivid and vital to several generations of readers

Mr. Darcy was writing, and Miss Bingley, seated near him, was watching the progress of his letter, and repeatedly calling off his attention by messages to his sister. Mr. Hurst and Mr. Bingley were at piquet, and Mrs. Hurst was observing their game. Elizabeth took up some needlework, and was sufficiently amused in attending to what passed between Darcy and his companion.

-- Jane Austen, *Pride and Prejudice*

The exact beginning of needlework is lost in the lapse of time. It is generally accepted as a fact that the art of embroidery had its origin among the Phrygians. Whether this is true or not, it is certain that the custom of decorating hangings and draperies with embroidery dates far beyond of the Christian era. Troy had its cunning workers in this art. Sidon gained great celebrity on account of the marvelous beauty of the embroidery executed by its women. The Greeks were skilled in such work, and the Moguls hung their walls with rich draperies, and covered their divans with the most gorgeous combination of wrought work and precious stones.

Time was nothing and labor did not enter into the discussion when a fine specimen of embroidery was to be produced. The work, while perhaps not a labor of love in many cases, was nevertheless inspired by a sentiment not unlike that which has always prompted the best work of human hands.

Needlework has a long tradition of women's occupations in England. A man could be a tailor, and sew outer clothing for other men, but there was no other male occupation that involved holding a needle. These role models were so strongly etched that "needle" became a symbol for a woman. In the *Memoir of Jane Austen*, her nephew testified to his aunt's skill as a needlewoman.

A group of women engaging in lively chatter as they happily sew is not a picture of which Mary Wollstonecraft would have approved. If a female was sewing, chances are she was inside the house, sedentary, and (thankfully) not reading novels. Refusal to engage in needlework was seen as female insurrection and a refusal to accept one's ordained station in life. Mary Wollstonecraft saw instruction in needlework as an indication of the intentional limiting of girls' intellectual development.

Needlework was a domestic occupation divided into categories with sociological implications. Plain sewing, for garments and items for household use, was viewed differently than embroidery, which had only a decorative function. The plain sewing of clothes was usually done in the mornings and the public face of needlework, embroidery, was accomplished in the evenings, on Sundays or when there was company.

Daughters of nobles certainly had time for decorative sewing, and in the eighteenth and nineteenth centuries, the popularity of embroidery began to descend to the ranks of daughters of the gentry and yeomanry classes. It was a social statement that these young women had the same leisure time as daughters of dukes to produce attractive pieces of needlework.

"Samplers" became the preferred illustration of a girl's skill in embroidery. Originally, "samplers" were just that, pieces of cloth on which women would practice a new stitch, in order to document it for future reference. Eventually, samplers became pieces of linen, illustrated with a variety of stitches, perhaps the alphabet, perhaps a biblical verse, perhaps scene from nature, to show just how capable at needlework, and by implication, how virtuous and conforming, the individual who made the sampler was at needlework, and, symbolically, at running a household. The sampler was often framed and displayed in a public room in the house for all, including potential suitors, to admire.

The popularity of samplers fueled a cottage industry, with women hired out as teachers of embroidery, shops that produced and sold the patterns, silks, yarns, and other requirements of that and other leisure pastimes popular in England, such as shellwork, and carpenters who made the tambour frames that would hold the embroiderer's work in progress.

Samplers became less popular beginning in the 1830s with the introduction of Berlin wool-work. This yarn was thick and in vivid colors, and one could quickly sew a bold, three-dimensional piece of work. This helped fuel the Victorian crazy to embroider everything, including bellpulls, piano legs coverings, caps, firescreens, and everything else that could be held still long enough to be poked with a needle.

In drawing up this little book of *Needlework Patterns in the Era of Jane Austen,* we understand in this modern age, many women do not have the same leisure time to produce attractive pieces of needlework as the daughters of dukes of yesteryear. Nor can we pretend to give technical directions that would enable a beginning needlewoman to teach herself this art. We have sought, therefore, only to provide the needlework patterns published in Ackermann's *Repository of Arts* during the time of Jane Austen.

A BORDER & a PATTERN of a VEIL.

November 1811

PATTERN for NEEDLE WORK.

December 1811

January 1812

N.°38 by R.Ackermann's Repository of Arts &c.Feb.1.1812, at 101 Strand London.

Plate 11. Vol.7

February 1812

N° 39 of R. ACKERMANN'S REPOSITORY of ARTS &c. Pub. 1 March 1812, at 101 Strand London.

March 1812

PATTERNS for NEEDLEWORK.

May 1812

PATTERNS for NEEDLEWORK.

June 1812

July 1812

PATTERN FOR NEEDLEWORK.

August 1812

September 1812

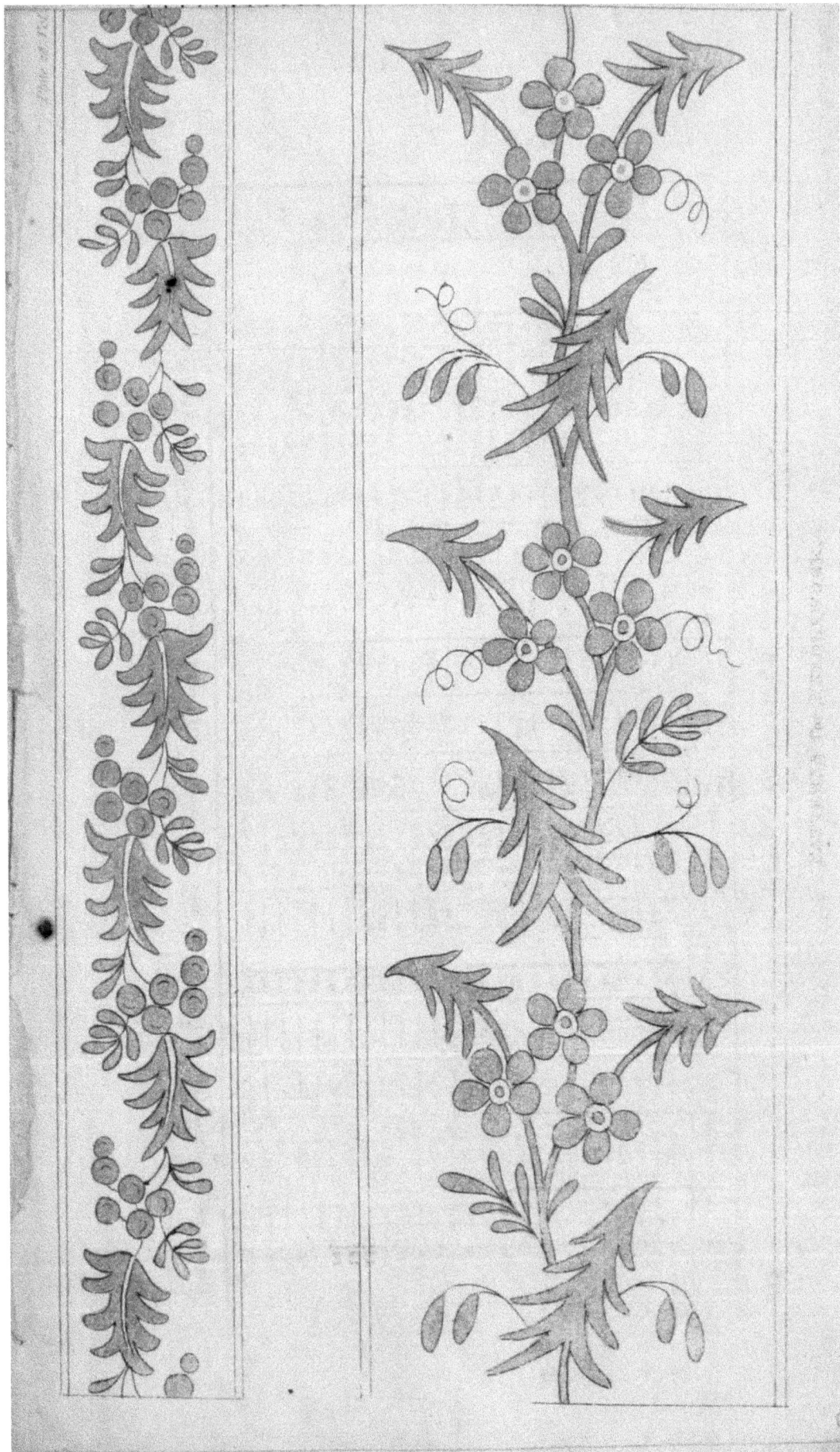

October 1812

November 1812

PATTERNS for NEEDLEWORK.

December 1812

PATTERNS FOR NEEDLEWORK.

January 1813

BORDERS for NEEDLEWORK.

February 1813

PATTERN FOR NEEDLEWORK.

March 1813

PATTERN FOR NEEDLEWORK.

June 1813

July 1813

HALF A COLLAR.

Nº 79 at R. Ackermann's Repository of Arts &c. Pub. Jan. 1 1814, at 101 Strand, London.

January 1814

Plate XV.

NEEDLEWORK PATTERNS.

February 1814

NEEDLEWORK PATTERNS.

Pub.d March 1844. at R. Ackermann's Repository of Arts &c. 101 Strand.

March 1814

April 1814

NEEDLEWORK PATTERNS

May 1814

July 1814

August 1814

NEEDLEWORK PATTERN.

September 1814

October 1814

November 1814

NEEDLEWORK PATTERN.

February 1815

NEEDLEWORK PATTERNS.

March 1815

NEEDLEWORK PATTERNS.

April 1815

June 1815

NEEDLEWORK PATTERNS.

July 1815

NEEDLEWORK PATTERN.

August 1815

NEEDLEWORK PATTERN.

September 1815

Pl. 26. Vol.XII

October 1815

November 1815

NEEDLEWORK PATTERNS.

Pub. by Tegg at Robinsons. 169. Strand.

December 1815

MUSLIN PATTERNS.

January 1816

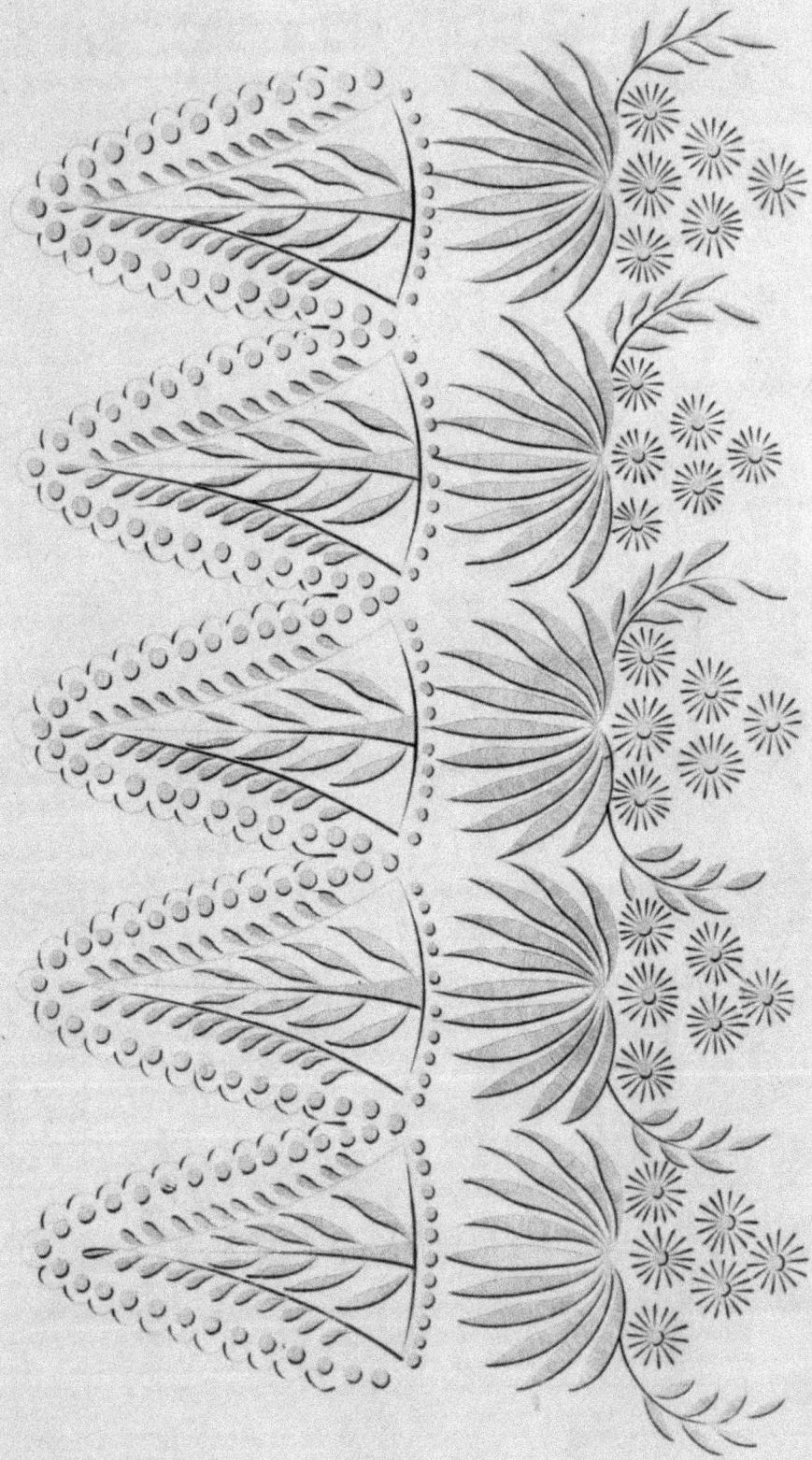

MUSLIN PATTERN.

February 1816

Pl.28 Vol.I

MUSLIN PATTERNS

March 1816

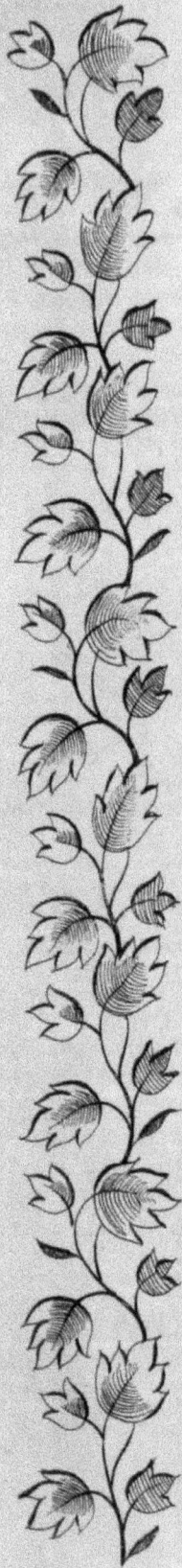

MUSLIN PATTERNS

April 1816

MUSLIN PATTERNS.

May 1816

Plate 2. Vol 1.

MUSLIN PATTERNS.

June 1816

MUSLIN PATTERN

July 1816

August 1816

Plate 7.

MUSLIN PATTERNS.

September 1816

October 1816

MUSLIN PATTERNS.

Published Nov.r 1816 at R. Ackermann's 101 Strand.

November 1816

NEEDLEWORK PATTERNS.

March 1817

MUSLIN PATTERNS.

April 1817

Pl. II. Vol IV

NEEDLEWORK PATTERNS.

August 1817

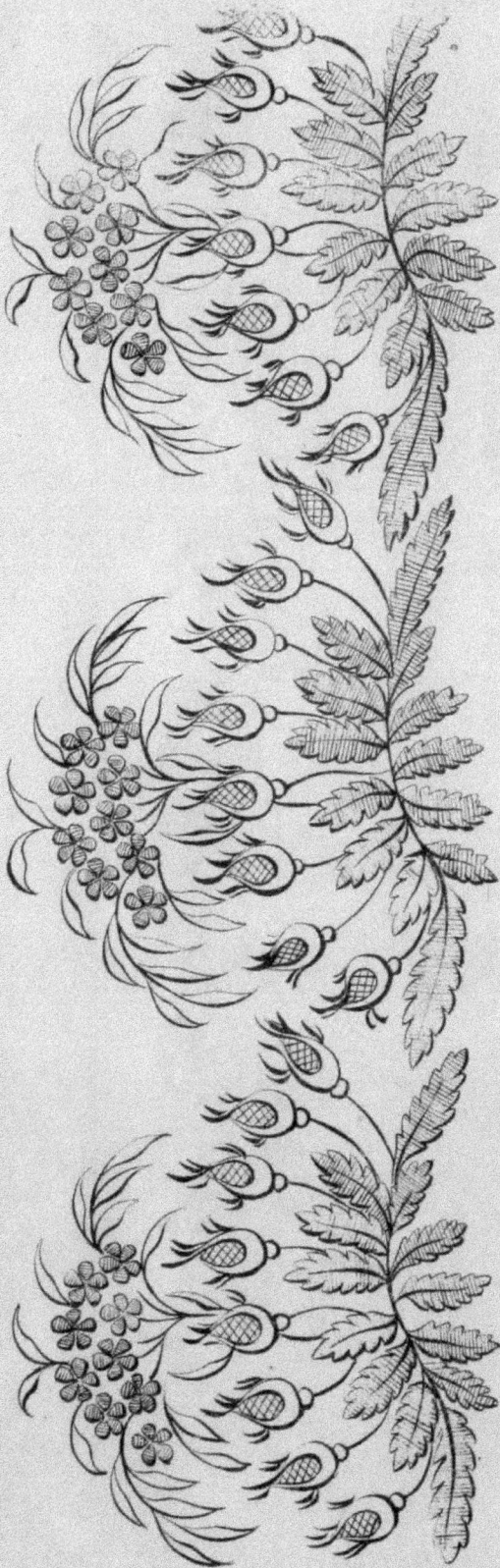

September 1817

Vol 4. Plate 23

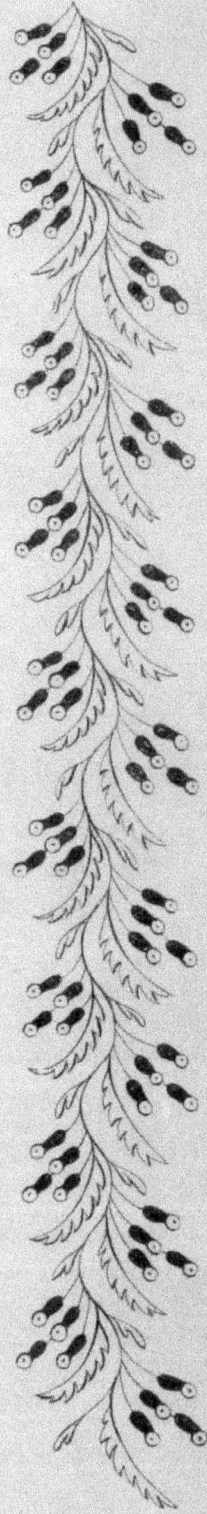

MUSLIN PATTERNS

October 1817

Fi 4. Plate 29

November 1817

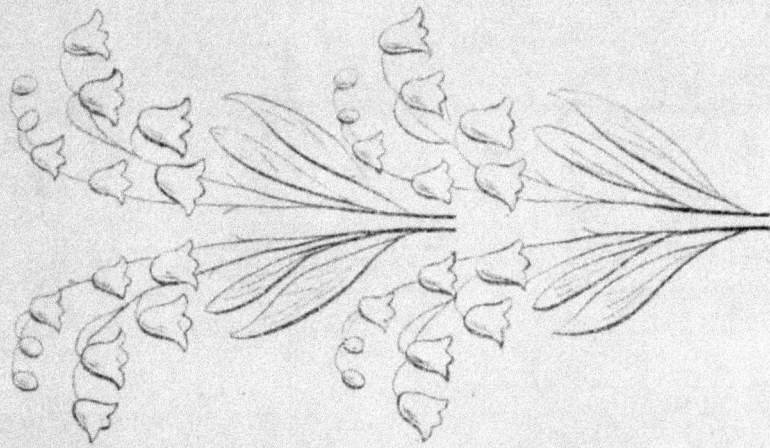

Muslin Patterns

December 1817

Plate 13 Vol.

MUSLIN PATTERNS

March 1818

MUSLIN PATTERNS.

April 1818

MUSLIN PATTERNS

June 1818

Plate 6. Vol. 6.

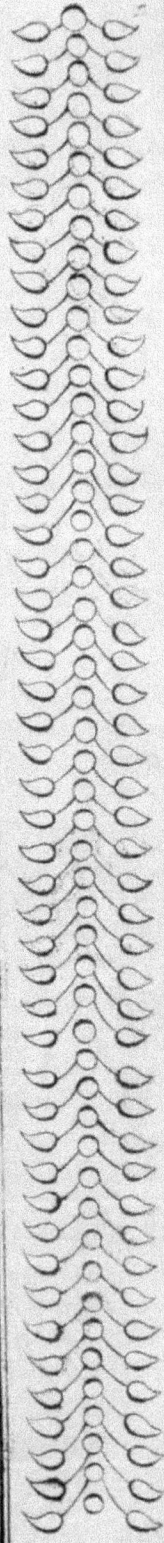

MUSLIN PATTERNS

July 1818

Plate 12. Vol 6

MUSLIN PATTERNS

August 1818

Plate 18 Vol 6

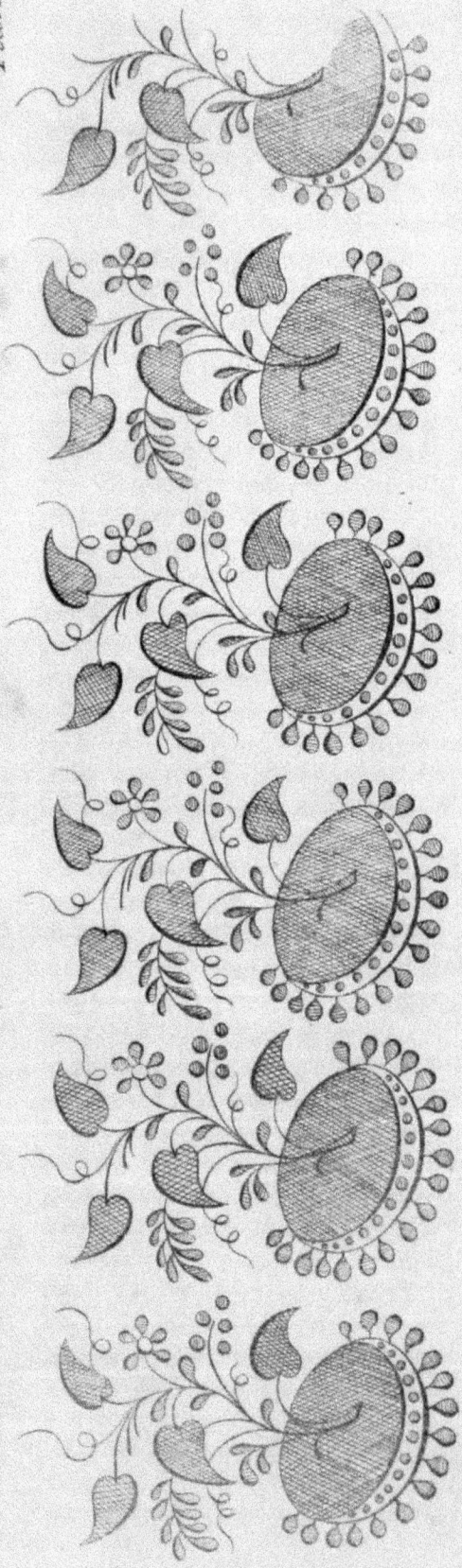

MUSLIN PATTERNS

Plate 116

MUSLIN PATTERNS

October 1818

MUSLIN PATTERNS

DECEMBER 1818

Plate 12 vol 7

MUSLIN PATTERNS.

February 1819

Plate Ns 1

MUSLIN PATTERNS

March 1819

MUSLIN PATTERNS.

May 1819

MUSLIN PATTERNS.

June 1819

Plate 8

MUSLIN PATTERN

August 1819

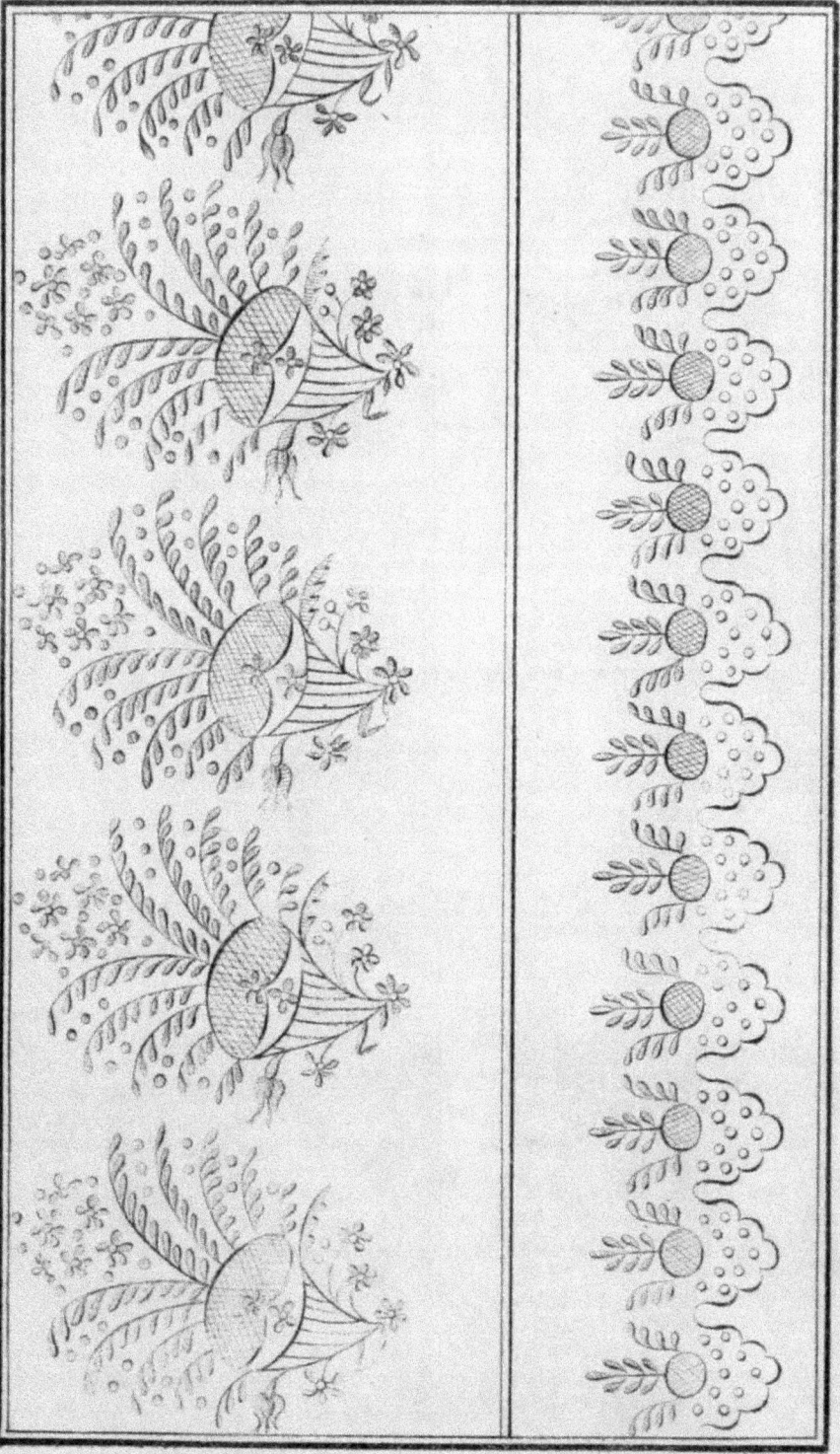

Plate 31. Vol. 8

MUSLIN PATTERNS

November 1819

Plate 12 vol 9

MUSLIN PATTERN

February 1820

Plate 18 Vol 9

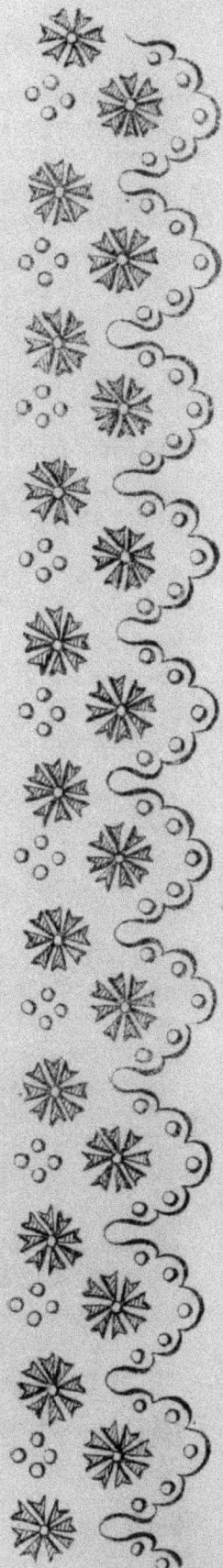

MUSLIN PATTERNS

March 1820

Plate 24 Fil. 9.

April 1820

Plate 3. Vol. 12.

MUSLIN PATTERN.

June 1820

Plate 50 Vol.10

MUSLIN PATTERNS.

November 1820

Needlework Publications on Archive.org

Web addresses change frequently, and many sources can appear in multiple places on the Internet. To avoid frustration due to the potential for broken links, search the internet via title or author for any reference you want to find. If you want the actual web address I used, it can be found below, if it's still available.

Christie, G. (1921). *Samplers and Stitches: A handbook of the Embroiderer's Art*. London: B.T. Batsford Ltd. https://archive.org/details/cu31924014066249

Frost, Annie S. (1877). The Ladies' Guide to Needle Work, Embroidery, etc. Being a Complete Guide to all Kinds of Ladies' Fancy Work. New York: H.T. Williams. https://archive.org/details/ladiesguidetonee00fros

Lefébure, E. (1888). *Embroidery and Lace: Their Manufacture and History from the Remotest Antiquity to the Present Day. A Handbook for Amateurs, Collectors, and General Readers*. London: H. Grevel. https://archive.org/details/embroiderylaceth00lefb

Potts, A.P. (1895). The Needle Workers' Guide without a Teacher. Chicago: W.T. Langton. https://archive.org/stream/needleworkersgui01pott#page/n3/mode/2up

Pullan, . (1859). *The Lady's Manual of Fancy Work: A Complete Instructor in Every Variety of Ornamental Needle-Work*. New York: Dick & Fitgerald. https://archive.org/details/ladysmanualoffan1859pull

Ruutz-Rees, J. E. (1881). *Home decoration: Art Needle-Work and Embroidery; Painting on Silk, Satin, and Velvet; Panel-Painting; and Wood-Carving*. New York: D. Appleton and Company. https://archive.org/details/homedecorationar00ruut

Townsend, W. G. P., & Pesel, L. F. (1908). *Embroidery: Or, The craft of the Needle*. New York: F.A. Stokes Company. https://archive.org/details/embroideryorcraf00town

JODY GAYLE, bestselling author and researcher, likens her work to that of a literary archeologist rather than a traditional author or imperator of history. She is dedicated to unearthing publications of the past, and sharing these long-forgotten books... the jewels and riches of the written word. She has uncovered tens of thousands of old publications from the eighteenth and nineteenth centuries and wants to bring them to life, and send her readers traveling back in time.

About Jody...

* She grew up on a farm in a small town of about 500 people and first learned to drive on a tractor. She can milk a cow as easily as pluck a chicken.

* Stood within twenty feet of the first node of the International Space Station. Unfortunately, her feet were firmly planted on the earth at the time.

* Has gone whitewater rafting and horseback riding in the mountains of Montana. She has swum with dolphins and sharks, and refueled a fighter jet in the sky on an Air Force KC135. Jody is a bit of an adventurer.

* Jody and her son share the same birthday -- New Year's Day!

She loves to hear from her readers. Visit her website and Facebook page.

Thank you for reading
FASHIONS IN THE ERA OF JANE AUSTEN

If you enjoyed this book, I would appreciate it if you'd help other readers enjoy it, too. After all, most books are purchased due to word-of-mouth recommendations. How can you help?

Recommend it. Please help other readers find this book by recommending it to friends, readers' groups, and discussion boards.

Review it. Please tell other readers why you liked this book by reviewing it on Amazon, Goodreads, or your blog. If you write a review, please send me a copy at jody@jodygayle.com